What the Evidence Shows

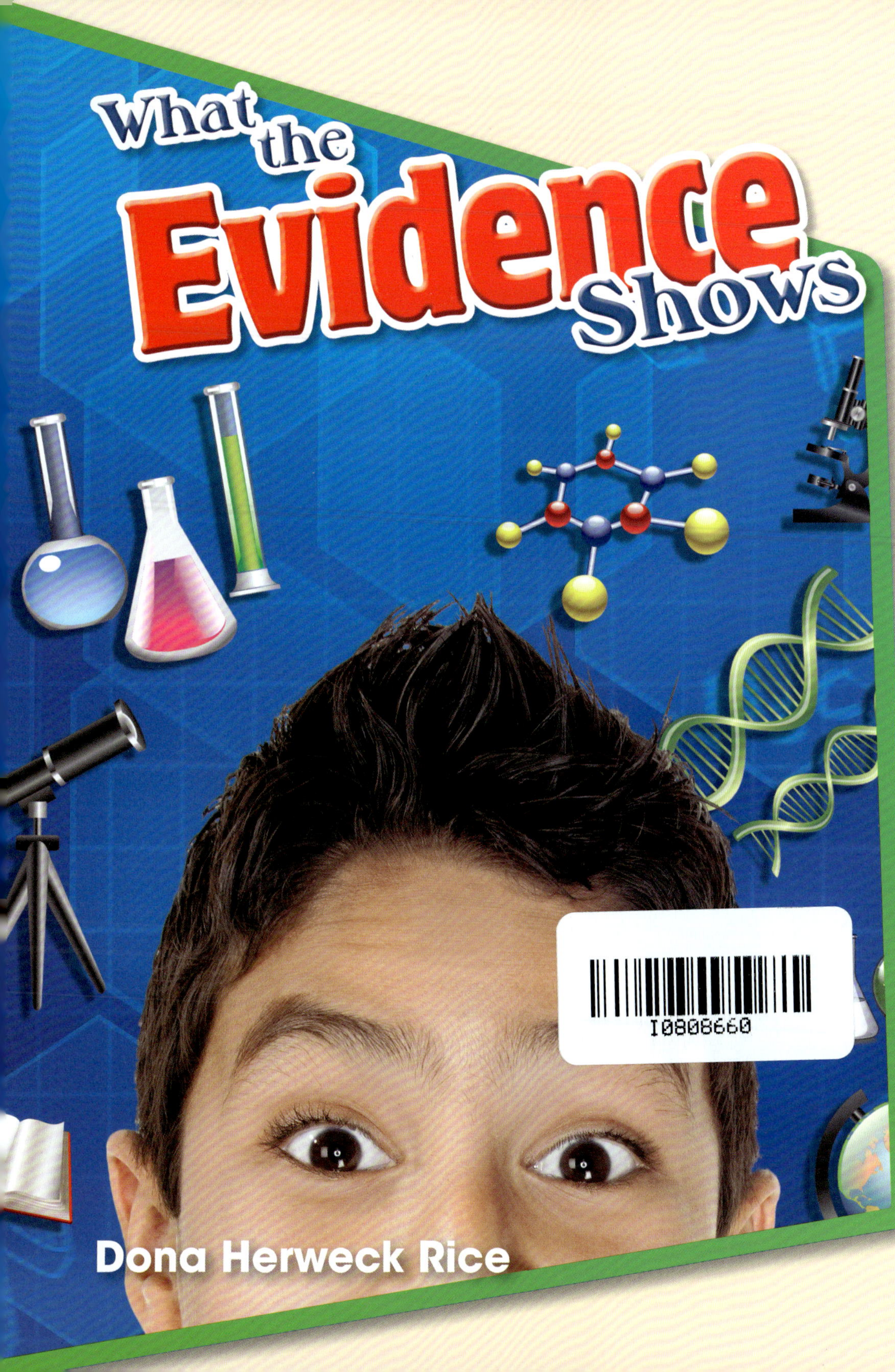

Dona Herweck Rice

Consultant

Leann Iacuone, M.A.T., NBCT, ATC
Riverside Unified School District

Publishing Credits

Rachelle Cracchiolo, M.S.Ed., *Publisher*
Conni Medina, M.A.Ed., *Managing Editor*
Diana Kenney, M.A.Ed., NBCT, *Content Director*
Dona Herweck Rice, *Series Developer*
Robin Erickson, *Multimedia Designer*
Timothy Bradley, *Illustrator*

Image Credits: Cover-p1 (background) Arshinov/Andrey/iStock, (front) Griessel/Creatista/iStock; p.2 (background) iStock; p.4 (illustration) iStock; p.6 (bottom) iStock; p.7 (illustration) Timothy Bradley; p.8-9 iStock; p.10 iStock; p.11 (top illustration) iStock, (bottom illustration) INSERT ILLUSTRATOR NAME HERE; p.12 (illustration) iStock; p.13-15 iStock ; p.16-17 chart based on: www.understandingscience.org. © 2007 University of California Museum of Paleontology, Berkeley, and the Regents of the University of California; p.18-27 (illustration) iStock; pp.28-29 (illustrations) Timothy Bradley; p.31-32 (illustrations) iStock; Back cover (illustration) iStock; all other images from Shutterstock.

Library of Congress Cataloging-in-Publication Data

Rice, Dona, author.
What the evidence shows / Dona Herweck Rice.
pages cm
Summary: "Scientists start with a question. They conduct experiments and gather data. But then what? Scientists must carefully analyze all the information to form a conclusion. They must go where the evidence leads them."-- Provided by publisher.
Audience: Grades 4 to 6
Includes index.
ISBN 978-1-4807-4730-2 (pbk.)
1. Science--Methodology--Juvenile literature. 2. Scientists--Juvenile literature. I. Title.
Q175.2.R535 2016
507.2'1--dc23

2015003157

Teacher Created Materials
5301 Oceanus Drive
Huntington Beach, CA 92649-1030
http://www.tcmpub.com

ISBN 978-1-4807-4730-2

Printed by: 590835
Printed in: China

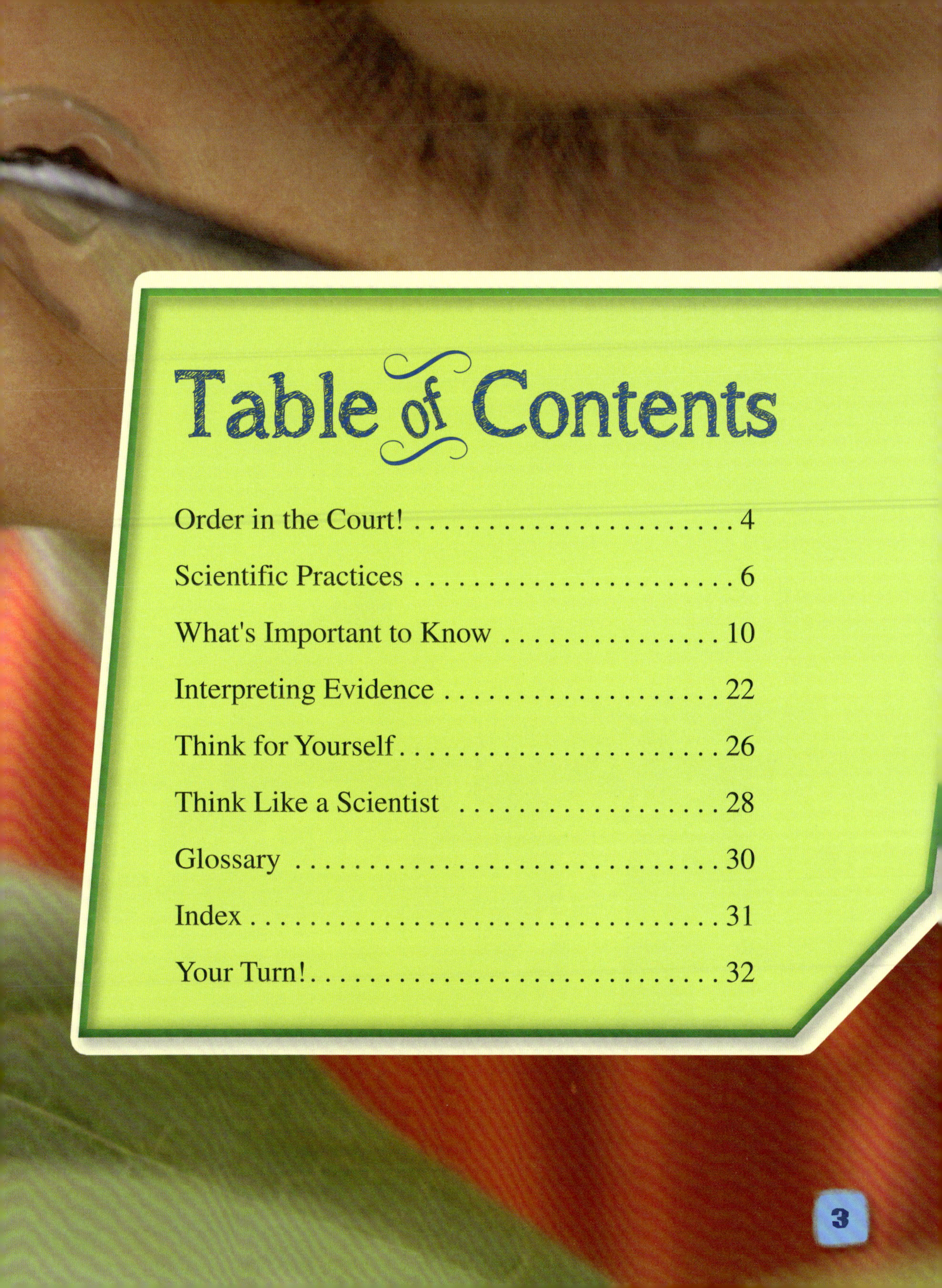

Table of Contents

Order in the Court!

"Ladies and gentlemen of the jury, the **evidence** clearly shows...."

If you've watched a courtroom television show, you've heard that phrase. Lawyers on each side present evidence to support their side of the case. Of course, they *want* to show only the evidence that's in their favor. Who wouldn't want to? It's their job to prove their side of the story. So, if evidence proving otherwise somehow mysteriously disappears...huh. How could that happen? Go figure! (Wink, wink.)

Well, evidence in a television courtroom is one thing, but evidence in the real world—the world of science—is quite another thing altogether. There is <u>no way</u> to make scientific evidence disappear. And no scientist is trying to prove anything. (It's not in the job description.) It's all about what the evidence shows—ALL the evidence. The evidence is just WHAT IT IS and can't be changed, twisted, rejected, or overlooked. In fact, the evidence is in the law itself—the laws of science—and these laws cannot be broken!

Scientists don't want to twist the truth: they want to find it. They don't want to manipulate facts; they want to get them straight. They don't want to miss any detail. They work with focus and determination until every detail has been discovered, logged, studied, **analyzed**, tested, and tested again.

If scientists had their own television dramas, the shows would never end. There's always more evidence to be found!

The word *evidence* comes from the Latin word *evidentia*, meaning "clearness."

Scientific Practices

Every good scientist follows essential practices in his or her work. These are SCIENCE DOs (as opposed to SCIENCE DON'Ts). In fact, experts say there are eight main science practices*, listed here:

1. **Asking questions**
2. **Developing and using models**
3. **Planning and carrying out investigations**
4. **Analyzing and interpreting data**
5. **Using mathematics and computational thinking**
6. **Constructing explanations**
7. **Engaging in argument from evidence**
8. **Getting, evaluating, and communicating information**

**Adapted from the Next Generation Science Standards, Appendix F, April 2013*

Science Don't

What's the worst thing you can do in science? Stop thinking for yourself. A good scientist questions everything!

Scientific evidence is an important part of every one of those practices. Take a look at them again, and you'll see that evidence is a very big deal! If you are going to ask a scientific question, you've probably seen some evidence that prompted you to think of the question. If you are going to develop a scientific model, you need quality evidence for that. If you are going to construct an explanation, you'll be explaining the evidence.

Science and evidence are very good friends! Scientists know that evidence is essential and that they can't just make up stuff, jump to conclusions, or take what someone else says and think, "Well, sure, if you say so!" Scientists dig in to find out for themselves so they can be sure that all evidence is good evidence, that it is accurate, and that it is complete.

Imagine that you want to play a game of basketball, and although you have never played before, everyone tells you what a great game it is. So, you grab a basketball and find a pickup game. A group of kindergarten kids is playing on the nearest court, and you ask them if they want to play. "Wow!" you think. "I'm fantastic at this game! I'm totally beating these kids! It's like I'm a basketball-playing machine!" After all, the evidence clearly shows that you are an awesome player, right? You're unstoppable, and it's as if you were born to play the game!

A Constant

Whenever conducting an experiment in which there is a comparison, scientists use something called a constant. A constant does not change. Things being compared are tested against something that is the same for both of them. That is the only way to be able to test a difference.

So, the next day, feeling pretty good about your skills, you head to the court again, where this time you find the New York Knicks shooting some hoops. You ask if you can play, too, and they say, "Sure, kid!" But, ouch! It's sooooo not like yesterday. You get creamed, slaughtered, demoralized, and pulverized. "Man, I'm the worst player ever," you wail. "I can't even get my hands on the ball!"

Of course, in both cases, you're wrong. The evidence is incomplete, and it's not based on anything consistent. All you know is that you have a good chance of beating kindergartners at basketball and that the Knicks are much better players than you are.

What's Important to Know

No matter who you are, there are some important rules to follow when it comes to gathering good evidence. These rules must be followed EVERY TIME. That means you, mister! (Hey, I saw you over there, trying to cut corners.) In science, you can't get away with shoddy work and spotty evidence. You've got to play by the rules; otherwise, everyone loses. Especially science.

A scientist looks for scientific evidence of a substance existing in a sample.

Don't make science **angry**. You wouldn't like science when it's **angry**.

(Okay, okay, just kidding. Science actually has a very pleasant personality. Just try it and you'll find out for yourself!) You will probably hear many people claim they have scientific evidence to argue for whatever it is they want to prove. And then there are other people who claim they have scientific evidence against whatever the first group wants to prove. Either way, just saying "scientific evidence" isn't evidence of anything other than the ability to pronounce "scientific evidence." **Authentic** scientific evidence means something. Above all, it means **reliability**. You can count on it.

Read on to find out how a scientist gets authentic scientific evidence.

Objectivity

"I wonder…" is a common thought for any good scientist. He or she always wonders "what if," "how come," and "what would happen." Scientists would be the first ones to tell you they don't know the answers to questions. They are the ones who ask the questions. And once they find an answer, they just keep on asking.

It's more than just being curious (which is a very good thing to be, by the way). It's being an inquirer—someone who never settles on, "Okay, here's the answer. Now I'll stop." But instead, the scientist says, "Okay, here are some interesting results. I'm going to study them some more and ask more questions."

Part of the reason why a scientist does this so well is because it's a scientist's job to keep an open mind, or to be **objective**. An objective person doesn't make judgments. The objective person plays fair and doesn't try to guess what will happen or force something to happen. The person's mind stays wide open so as not to miss anything because his or her brain was stuck on some other expectation.

environmentalist

archaeologist

Unbiased Results

Any time you see a scientific report that declares it is based on good research and evidence, be sure you know who did the research. Sometimes, companies that want to sell something pay for research that might support what they want to do. You can see why the evidence they get may not always be trustworthy.

Good Procedures

Scientists have long used something called the **scientific method**, and there's plenty that's great about it. Basically, the scientific method lists important steps in the process of conducting scientific study and research. At one time, people thought the steps had to come in sequence. They thought the steps were always the same. But we know now that's not the case. Science is a process. It leads the scientist in many different and unexpected directions. Science is not a recipe to be followed. It's an open-ended exploration of what can be proven. The steps you find in the scientific method are quite often part of that process, so it's still a good idea to learn about them. Take a look!

Today, when we think of the method for "doing" science, we see it as an open-ended process that includes the practices mentioned on the right. It doesn't have steps but rather **components** that make up good scientific practice. Interestingly, those components are mainly the same ones you find in the scientific method. *(Prediction? Good!* ✔ *Experimentation? Good!* ✔*)* We just think about the components a little differently than we used to.

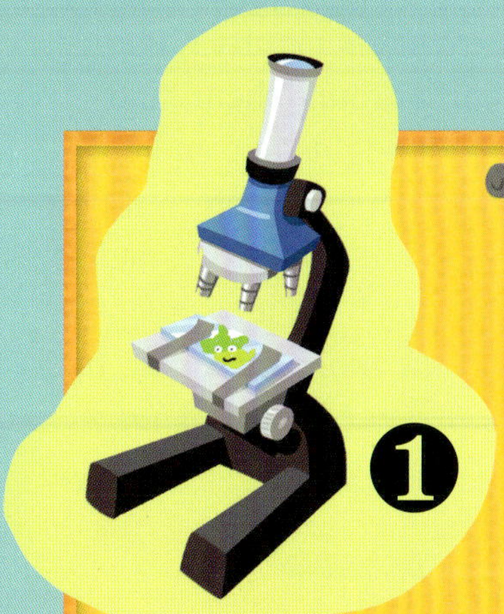

What's the Method?

These steps are common parts of the scientific method.

1. **observation and research**
2. **hypothesis**
3. **prediction**
4. **experimentation**
5. **analysis**
6. **reporting**

We know now that the heart of science is **inquiry**. What is inquiry? It's the multiple ways in which scientists investigate the world around them, find evidence, and pose explanations for what they **observe**. It begins like an itch that won't go away, right in the middle of your back. Stretch… stretch… almost there… got it! Ahhh. Oh, wait, there's another one! Stretch… stretch… and so it goes. And that, my friends, is the nature of scientific inquiry! An idea creeps up on you, and it grabs your attention. You think on it, and the more you think, the more you need to know. *What would happen if…? How can I know? What has already been learned? What can I add to it?*

This is how great inquiry begins.

Once a scientist has the itch, he or she starts to explore, make observations, ask questions, and research what others have done and learned. This is determined partly by what the scientist is trying to discover and partly by the discoveries other scientists make along the way that redirect them in new and surprising directions.

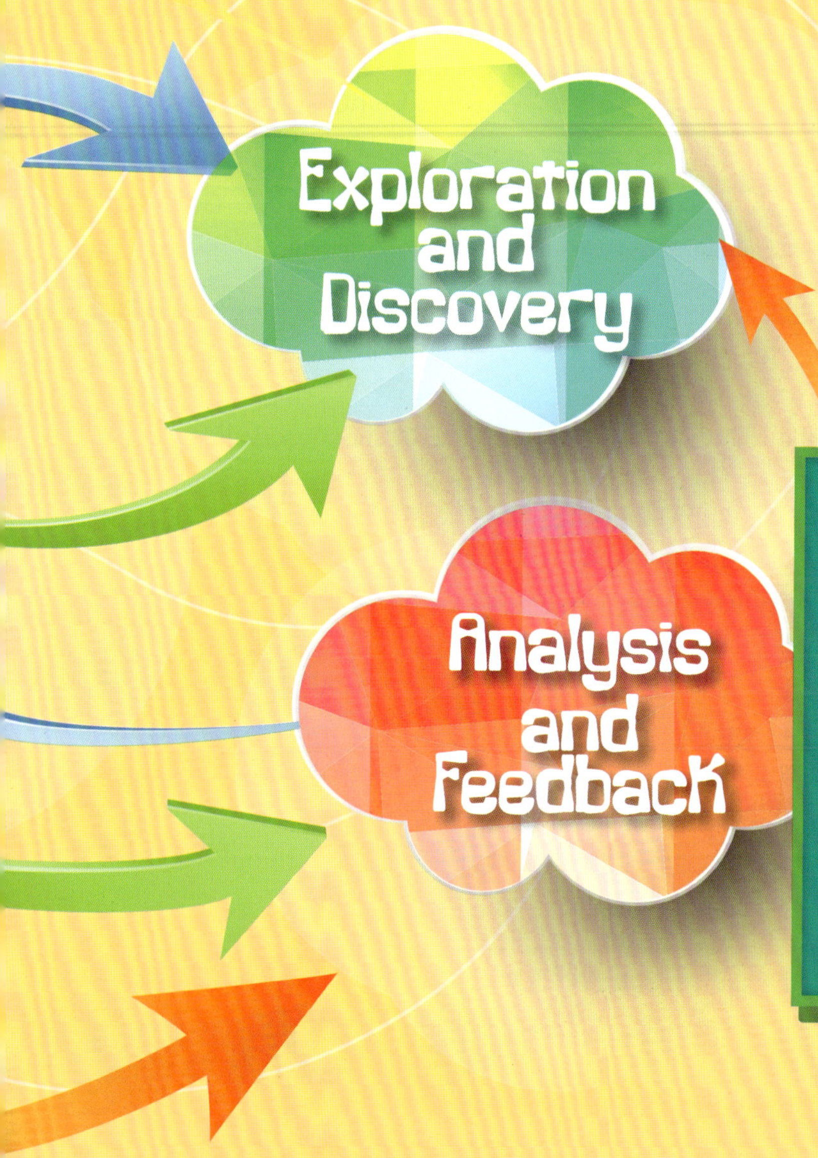

Does Anyone Have a Map?

The path of inquiry is not a straight line. It's circuitous, meaning that it loops and circles and changes as new things are discovered and new questions come up. There's no road map. It's a journey of discovery!

A scientist analyzes data on a computer.

Almost always, it's not just one scientist conducting research but instead a whole team of scientists. Good science involves teamwork!

TEST

Whatever the scientist is investigating, he or she must decide that the ideas are **testable** in order to move forward. If not, there is no science. Testing is a must; so, while exploring, the scientist begins to test. The testing might be in a lab, but it might also be wherever the testing makes most sense. Maybe it's in a forest, maybe it's underwater, or maybe it's on a computer. There's no single rule about this!

While testing, the scientist crafts a reasonable explanation for the question at the heart of the inquiry. The scientist gathers and interprets data on everything he or she observes. While doing this, the scientist continues to adapt and change his or her thinking according to the findings.

A good scientist also analyzes everything. That's right—everything! He or she asks questions about the findings and data and repeats the tests. The scientist checks and double checks. In order to be accurate, the tests must be repeatable and the scientist must get the same result EVERY TIME.

ANALYZE

A scientist gathers and tests samples from a forest.

A scientist conducts tests in a lab.

Acceptance

When a scientist works, he or she doesn't keep their work quiet. The scientist shares his or her work with other scientists, and they experiment, too, to see if they get the same or different results. When others review the scientist's work, they either accept it or reject it. If most experts accept it, the work is considered "good science," and it begins to be used to support other inquiries.

And on and on it goes.

No Secrets

If no one else is allowed to test something that a single group of scientists test, any so-called evidence is not good science. Good science is always public and testable.

Consensus

It is very hard for a group of people to reach perfect agreement on anything. Think about the times that you and your friends try to agree on what to do. In science, as long as the majority agrees and just a few don't—even if the dissenters are loud and insistent—we consider it a consensus.

Acceptance of a scientist's work depends on the evidence that supports it. Other scientists have to be able to test it and get the same results. They have to see that the evidence is valid and accurate. Science experts must reach **consensus**, which means they have to agree on approving the work.

Of course, not everyone has to agree. Let's face it, there will always be those people who just like to make a fuss and disagree with things. Some won't like the results, or they might have their own ideas about how things should go. The scientist doesn't have to do anything to get those people to agree. But good science should hold up when objective scientists check it out.

A student tests a robot to find evidence to support an idea.

Lines of Evidence

Good evidence is derived from several lines of evidence. Each line comes from a different type of test. The more lines of evidence there are to support an idea, the more strongly we can accept it.

Interpreting Evidence

What does it all mean? To figure it out, the scientist has to use his or her most important tool: brainpower! The evidence does not paint a picture all on its own. It has to be put together like a puzzle. All the puzzle pieces on their own don't mean anything. They are just a jumble, and they need to be organized and pieced together to make meaning. A scientist studies the evidence like pieces of a puzzle and puts the evidence together to make meaning.

Students test and gather evidence about engineering.

Empirical Evidence

Scientists look for empirical evidence. That is evidence found through observation and experiments.

What if there are missing pieces? A good scientist tests some more to find those pieces. What if the scientist doesn't know that there are missing pieces? That's why we say that nothing is ever proven or disproven, because more pieces of the puzzle can be discovered at any time. Science does not prove ideas, and it doesn't disprove them either. It accepts or rejects ideas based on evidence. Accepted and rejected ideas can be changed as new evidence becomes available.

Hey, wait a minute! Isn't science all about facts? Nope, it's about evidence. A good scientist would never say that something is a fact with 100 percent certainty. There is no way for us to know anything about the natural world with 100 percent certainty. We can have thousands of pages of good evidence, but still no good scientist would say the idea is proven. It's accepted, not proven.

But hold on! This IS NOT SAYING that science is guesswork. Far from it! Painstaking research, testing, questioning, and analysis go into scientific practice. But we know that no matter what, there can always be more evidence to find.

Take, for example, the atom. For a very long time, scientific study showed that the atom was the smallest unit of matter, but in the early 20th century, further study discovered protons, neutrons, and electrons in atoms. Moreover, now we know that there are even smaller particles such as charmed quarks and neutrinos. Who knows what else we will discover in the future? Tiny villages of Whos living inside atoms? (Okay, that's not likely, but it's fun to think about, isn't it?)

The idea of black holes has been accepted for years. Recently, Stephen Hawking proposed new ideas concerning this topic.

Expected vs. Observed

When testing, a scientist sets expectations as to what will be observed and compares those expectations to what is *actually observed*.

Scientists attached depth recorders to these Steller sea lions to learn how deep they dive.

Scientists will observe and analyze data from this elephant seal's transmitter to learn about its migratory habits.

Think for Yourself

You now know what you need to do when finding your own scientific evidence. (Explore. ✔ Test. ✔ Analyze. ✔ Share with others and let them test ✔.) But do you know what to do when you are presented with someone else's evidence? How do you know if you can trust it? Is it objective and unbiased? Did it follow good procedures? Have other experts accepted it?

When considering evidence and its validity, you should always know where it came from. Who found the evidence and who paid for the research? How strong is the evidence? Can you get more information about the evidence?

You should always stop and think about the evidence in front of you. Don't always believe what someone tells you. Especially don't always believe what you read on the Internet.

You should also be sure that most scientists talk about the evidence in the same way. For example, if you read evidence in one report and it says that Santa Claus is jolly because he listens to Pharrell's "Happy" while driving his sleigh, but all other experts say that Santa is jolly because he thinks happy thoughts while riding in his sleigh…well, Santa may *like* Pharrell, but the first researcher has clearly put a spin on things.

Okay, okay, there's no evidence about why Santa is jolly. At least there's plenty of evidence that Santa exists, right?*

Think Like a Scientist

How can you think like a great scientific inquirer? Experiment and find out!

What to Get

- board or ramp
- clay
- gravel
- potting soil
- sand

What to Do

1. Choose a question:
   - **a.** Which soil type will slide most easily when it is wet? Hint: Test each soil type using the same amount of water for each test.
   - **b.** At what angle do different soil types slide most easily? Hint: Test each soil type at the same height; retest at a different height.

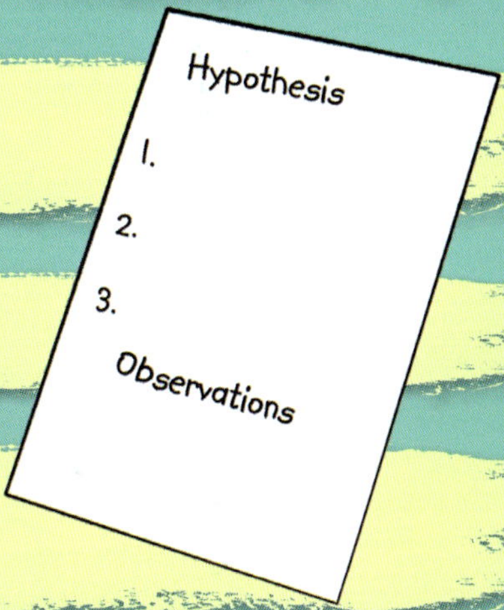

2. Using the question and what you know about soils, formulate a hypothesis.
3. Design an experiment to test your hypothesis.
4. Write the steps to your experiment and record your observations.
5. Create a record of your experiment and the results. What is the answer to the question? What did you learn from this experiment? How do your results compare to those of your classmates?

Glossary

analyzed—studied things to learn about their parts, what they do, and how they relate to other things

authentic—real, not copied

components—parts of something

computational thinking—logical problem solving that is similar to the way a computer analyzes and resolves problems

consensus—an idea or opinion that is shared by all the people in a group

constant—something that stays the same

data—information used to calculate, analyze, or plan something

evaluating—determining the value of something in a careful and thoughtful way

evidence—something that shows that something else exists or is true

inquiry—process of questioning, investigating, and testing

interpreting—explaining and understanding something

objective—based on facts rather than feelings or opinions

observe—to watch and listen carefully

reliability—the quality or state of being trusted

scientific method—steps used by scientists to test ideas through experiments and observations

testable—able to be tested or worked on to the point of having a clear result

Index

YOUR TURN!

Finding Evidence

Look on the ground outside at a park or a playground and gather evidence as to what activities have recently been done there. Do you see footprints? Are they big or small? In what direction did the person walk? Challenge a friend to see who can find the most evidence.